Great Glen

The story of a
Leicestershire village

Max Wade-Matthews

Great Glen

The story of a

Leicestershire village

Max Wade-Matthews

**Heart of Albion
Press**

Great Glen
The story of a Leicestershire village
Max Wade-Matthews

Heart of Albion Press
ISBN 1 872883 49 4

British Library Cataloguing in Publication Data

A catalogue record for this book is available from the British
Library.

Printed in England by Addkey Print.

Heart of Albion Press
2 Cross Hill Close, Wymeswold,
Loughborough, LE12 6UJ

Contents

Chapter 1

The Early History of the Parish

The Iron Age and Roman Period

Great Glen, which lies some seven miles to the south-east of Leicester, boasts one of the oldest place names in the county. The name, from the Celtic *glennos*, meaning valley, was given to the area by the Corieltauvi, an Iron Age tribe that settled here before the Roman invasion. *Glennos* or *glenne* is believed to have originally referred to the Sence valley in general, before being incorporated into the name of the land-holdings that evolved into the present-day villages of Glen Magna and Glen Parva.

The Romans arrived in Britain in AD 43 and stayed for almost 400 years before the last troops finally left in 409. We can picture the British inhabitants of Glen staring with awe and wonderment as the exotic Roman legions marched along the *Via Devana*, the present day Gartree Road, to their base at *Ratae Coritanorum*, the modern Leicester. The road connected Colchester to Chester, and ran a little to the north of the present parish boundary, through the, now deserted, village of Stretton Magna, whose name significantly means 'the settlement on the Roman road'.

When the soldiers of the Leicester garrison came to the end of their service some returned home but others remained and settled into the civilian life of their adopted country. One such veteran and his family, whose names are now lost to history, settled in Glen and built a home on what is now the Recreation Ground. In 1962 evidence of this villa came to light when fragments of Samian ware and Roman tesserae were found. Four years later a fourth-century Roman coin was discovered, while in 1971 other fragments of Roman material were unearthed. In 1977, in the neighbouring parish of Burton Overy, thirty shards of Roman pottery were found some six hundred yards south-west of the Gartree Road. In 1995, evidence of Roman and Anglo-Saxon sites was found at Stretton Magna.

1

Anglo-Saxon Glen

From the third century Angles and Saxons, from what is now northern Germany and Denmark, began to drift into England, not so much as invaders, but more as peaceful immigrants. By the beginning of the seventh century most of England was controlled by the Anglo-Saxons who divided the country into a number of kingdoms. Glen became part of the kingdom of Mercia, an area which became Christian on the conversion of King Peada in about 655.

In Anglo-Saxon England there was not one royal capital, as there is today. The Anglo-Saxon kingdoms consisted of a number of royal estates that had to provide food for the royal household on one or more nights each year. Each of these estates included a large hall and usually a minster which served as the mother church for the surrounding area. There are three reasons for believing that Glen was the administrative centre of one such estate.

The outline of the present day parishes of Great Glen, Wistow, Stretton Parva and Stretton Magna.

The first is the evidence of the Anglo-Saxon names of the surrounding villages: Norton (meaning a settlement north of a more important centre) and Burton (a garrison probably built to defend an important site at the time of the Danish invasions). The royal estate, I believe, would have included both these as well as the two Strettons, Newton (the new settlement) and Wistow (Wistan's holy place).

The map of the present parishes of Great Glen, the two Strettons and Wistow, shows that the combined area is compact and probably would have formed one unit. Another interesting point to note is that in an itinerary of 1280 the modern parishes of Glen, Stretton, Burton and Norton were listed together.

2

Although the parish boundaries were determined by farming considerations - the need for shelter, water, grazing and arable land - the township of Great Glen, as with almost any other village, has not been, nor is, static. Roman and early Saxon Glen seems to have been centred in the Orchard Lane area, on the site of the present Co-op farm (Ordnance Survey grid reference SP655973). In 1990 Saxo-Norman pottery was found here as well as evidence of cob wall house foundations and what may have been a windmill mound.

The second reason is the early dedication of the church, one of the most southerly dedications to St Cuthbert, a missionary who was based on Lindisfarne (also known as Holy Island) Northumberland. On Cuthbert's death, in 687, he was buried on the island where his shrine became the spiritual centre of Northumbrian Christianity. In 867 Viking raids forced the monks to leave the island, taking Cuthbert's body with them. After 120 years of being carried over northern England the saint was finally laid to rest in what was to become Durham Cathedral.

Although there is no physical evidence of an Anglo-Saxon church at Glen, in the east wall of the north aisle are two fragments of Mercian sculpture. One may be a mutilated crucifix. The other, part of a figure holding a rod, is believed to be Christ healing a blind man. It is possible, but by no means provable, that these may be fragments of a, now vanished, *reredos* (carved panel behind the altar) and as such part of an important church.

A fragment of the Mercian carving now set into the east wall of the north aisle in St Cuthbert's church.

With the erection of a church, probably in the eighth century, a community of dwellings, possibly for the use of the priests who served the church, seems to have sprung up to the east of the present vicarage (SP653937). The medieval earthworks left by these buildings were visible until 1984 when new houses were built on the site.

The third reason for believing that Glen was an administrative centre is the evidence of a charter, issued from *Glenne* at the Mercian assembly of 849. This concerns a grant of land in Worchester from Ealhhun, Bishop of Worchester, to the Mercian King, Berhtwulf, 'so that he may be a better friend to him'. This was not the first time that meetings had been held in the area for previously they had been held at Gumley (749, 772 and 779), Leicester (803) and Croft Hill (836).

It is quite probable that it was at this assembly that Wistan was murdered. He was the grandson of Wiglaf, who had been the Mercian king from 827 to his death in 839. As Wistan's father, Wimund, had predeceased Wiglaf, the succession should have passed to Wistan. However, as he was a child, his uncle Berhtwulf was appointed regent. Berhtwulf's son, Brifardus, was an ambitious man who, wanting to assure his succession against the rightful heir, planned to marry Wistan's widowed mother, Elfleda, but as she was Brifardus's godmother she refused on the grounds that the marriage would have been contrary to church law.

Not undaunted, during the assembly, Brifardus invited the unsuspecting Wistan to a meeting. On greeting his cousin, Brifardus pulled out a hidden sword and, with the hilt, fatally struck the prince on the head. Wistan's body was taken to Repton monastery where it was buried with his father and grandfather. Berhtwulf was not among the signatories on the charter, so it is a matter of conjecture as to whether or not he knew of his son's plan. The site of the murder is remembered in the name of the church and settlement where it took place - Wistow. Possibly the royal residence was somewhere on the site of the present Wistow Hall, and Wistow church is on the site of a memorial chapel which was dedicated to the murdered prince, probably built on the site of the crime.

Danish Occupation

In 835, after enjoying 200 years free of invasion, the Anglo-Saxons' false illusion of calm and safety (they had neither warships nor coastal defences) was shattered when Danish longships raided Sheppey. Six years later Mercia itself was attacked when Lindsey suffered heavy damage. In 851 the Mercian army under Berhtwulf was put to flight when they tried to defend the mouth of the Thames from about 12,000 Danes who had arrived in 350 longships and taken Canterbury and London. In 873 Repton was captured, the monastery destroyed and a fortified area by the church became the Danish headquarters.

Statuette of Æthelflæd 'The Lady of the Mercians'. Originally built to surmount a fountain in Victoria Park and now on display in the City Rooms, Leicester.

In 877 the eastern area of Mercia, which included Glen, was invaded and soon after became part of the Danelaw. The Danes then turned from pillage to settlement and became absorbed into the existing society. Glen must have been near the limit of Danish influence for settlements named by the Danes are not so plentiful as in the north of Leicestershire. Such Danish names usually end in -by (the Danish equivalent of the Anglo-Saxon -ton) and include Oadby, Saulby and Frisby. Danelaw lasted until 919 when an army led by Ethelflæd, 'The Lady of the Mercians', granddaughter of King Alfred, defeated the Danes and took control of Leicester.

The Gartree Hundred

The concept of the shire emerged in the tenth century as a unit of administration represented by a *shire reeve*, a term which, over the years, has been contracted into the modern word 'sheriff'. The *shire reeve* was responsible for the gathering of taxes and the dispensing of justice. He was based on the main town from which the shire took its name. The shire was divided into hundreds which elected representatives who usually met every four weeks at a central point. The meetings, which were attended by one of the king's representatives, decided on taxation and were the main means of communication between the king and his subjects.

Glen was in the hundred of Gartree, the hundred court of which met by the Gartree Bush, near Shangton, where the Gartree Road was intersected by the Melton to Market Harborough Road, the modern B6047 (SP972717). This meeting place may well have been the source for the name *Gartree* which means in Old Norse the "scarred tree', which would have been an excellent landmark. Indeed there are examples of the same name being used in other areas of England and various parts of Sweden.

Domesday Book

The first reference to the population of Great Glen is found in the Domesday Book, which was compiled on the instructions of William the Conqueror in 1086, twenty years after his invasion of England. Although the book was intended as a record of the value of William's new territory and not as a demographic survey, it does give a rough idea of how many lived in Glen towards the end of the eleventh century. The Lord of the Manor was Hugh of Grandmesnil, custodian of Leicester Castle and the largest land owner in the county. Grandmesnil leased out the land to two sub-tenants: William Lovett, who held seventeen carucates and two bovates of land; and Alwin, who held only one carucate, a grand total of eighteen and a quarter carucates.

In Leicestershire, a duodecimal county, a carucate or ploughland (120 acres) was the fiscal unit for the taxation of land. The carucate (a name that derive from *caruca*, a heavy wheeled plough pulled by eight oxen, which cut deep furrows) contained four virgates, or yardlands. Half a virgate was called a bovate, or oxgang, which was the land of one ox. As well as this arable land there was a mill and thirty acres of meadow, making a total of 2,220 acres.

The survey records the village as having five slaves, two male and three female, who worked on the demesne land; fourteen villagers; six smallholders and twenty freemen. If we exclude the five slaves there is a total of forty, however, as this number does not include wives or children we can estimate that in 1086 the village had a population of about 200.

The Mediaeval Church

Although the Domesday survey does not mention a priest or a church this does not mean that there was not one in the village. Indeed, as we have seen, it is certain that there was one. Churches were only mentioned in the Domesday Book when they were taxable. As in so many other places the Normans, as a sign of their authority, pulled down the Anglo-Saxon church and rebuilt it in their own unique style. All that remains of this church is the Romanesque south door, which can be dated stylistically to about 1100, and the twelfth-century font.

During the reign of King Stephen (1135–1154) the church at Great Glen was appropriated by Ralph, Bishop of Lincoln, to the Abbot and Convent of Alcester, Warwickshire. In 1220 'according with a long standing custom' the vicar, Phillip, was paying the rector, Thomas, six marks a year,[1] receiving in return the whole rights of the living. The rector was also responsible for holding three services a week at the chapel at Stretton Magna, which, even in the thirteenth century, had a very small population.

1. *One mark (of silver) was equivalent to thirteen shillings and four pence (66 new pence).*

The main points of interest on the capitals of the church south door are the Romanesque equestrian carvings. Dating from about 1100, they were fortunately kept and replaced in their original position by the nineteenth century restorers.

7

In 1294 William Gilmeyn, one of the major land holders in Glen, granted to the abbey two virgates of land which until then had been held by William de Irees. In return for the land the abbey paid ten shillings a year to the manor of Newton Harcourt. In 1465, Edward IV, on finding that the abbey was 'quite run to decay, insomuch that for a long time there had been none in it but the abbot', transferred the church to Evesham Abbey.

Glen Martel

In the twelfth and thirteenth centuries Great Glen was known as Glen Martel, a designation which dated from the reign of Henry II (1154–1189) when Eudo Martel inherited the lordship. One of Martel's tenants was Philip, vicar of Glen, who held one virgate of land. On Philip's death, about 1247, this land was to have passed to his son William. However, apparently William was illegitimate, for in 1247 William Martel, grandson of Eudo and son and heir of Ivo, demanded the return of the land as Philip had died without a legal heir. There were, however, complications as William (Philip's son) told the court that he did not entirely hold the land for half of it belonged to one Geoffrey Pavey and another man, Philip, held one toft. In the event William Martel withdrew his suit.

That tax evasion was known in the thirteenth century can be seen from the antics of Peter Martel. In 1259 he transferred ten virgates of land in Quorn and Barrow to the Knights Templar under the condition that he was to continue to hold the land rent free. As property belonging to the Knights Templar was exempt from tax Martel was able to continue to occupy the land without any fiscal obligation.

William Martel was killed in 1265 fighting for Henry III against the army of Simon de Montfort at the Battle of Evesham. The records of William's estate at the time of his death show that he held about one quarter of the total land in Glen.

In 1272 Roger Martel, who with his brother Richard also held lands at Carlton and Mountsorrel, was granted the right to hold a market at Glen on Mondays and a yearly fair on the eve, day and morrow of St Cuthbert's Day (20 March). In 1348, when Henry Martel was lord of the manor, Edward III changed the weekly market day to Friday and the annual fair to the eve, day and morrow of the feast of SS Philip and James (1 May).

In 1280, on the death of Roger Martel, the eleven ploughlands, which he held from Roger de la Zouch, passed to his widow Joan. The following year Joan married de la Zouch, who held much of the rest of the land in the parish, including the mill and sixty acres of meadow. From this it will be noted that in the two hundred years since the Domesday survey an additional thirty acres of meadow had been formed. It is not clear whether this new meadow was from newly-cleared land or from former arable land near the river which had been put over to permanent pasture.

The Rebuilding of the Church

The church, with the addition of a north aisle, was rebuilt about 1320 by Roger Martel. That the east end of the aisle was used as a Lady Chapel we know from the redundant piscina, evidence which points to the presence of a pre-Reformation stone altar.

Another pointer to the original use of this aisle can be seen in the shafts of the arcade. Niches can still be seen where the screen which separated the aisle from the nave was fitted. These shafts can be architecturally dated to the early fourteenth century. The holes and cutaway stonework in the two arches at the end of the arcade show signs of the course of the staircase which led up to the rood loft which originally spanned the nave at this point. At the Reformation rood lofts, which were used for the candles and images that featured in the ritual of medieval Christian worship, were deemed superstitious and ordered to be taken down.

This aisle contained a chapel of some importance as the original east window contained medieval coloured glass. In 1622 this was described by the Leicester historian John Burton as: 'Gules, three marteaux, or claw-hammers, erect, Or. (Martel). Gules, a lion rampant queue fourche, Argent. (Montfort, Earl of Leicester). Gules, seven mascles voided and conjoined, Or. (Quincy). Gules, a cross portate Vert; between a crown of thorns Vert, a heart, a hand and a foot Argent, pierced Gules, a spear Or in bend. (An escutcheon devised to express the passion of Christ)'. Sad to say, when the window was repaired in 1796, the glass was found too decayed to be reused and was thrown away.

In the western face of the lower stage of the tower is the sole remaining complete window of the fourteenth century church. That the church had a tower in the fourteenth century is also clear from the evidence of the bell which was made by the Leicester founder John Stafford, who was working in the mid-fourteenth century. It originally bore the inscription: *Ista Camjana Facta Est In Honore Sci Cuthberti* (This bell is made in honour of St Cuthbert). In 1898 this ancient bell was recast and now bears an inscription in memory of Charles Packe who died in 1896.

Descent of the Manor

Henry Martel succeeded to the lordship in 1333 while still a minor. On his death in 1352 there was some confusion over the owner of the land which he had held. On enquiry, however, it was found that he had held no land of the king and the Leicestershire escheator was ordered not to 'intermeddle further in the manor of Glen Magna' and to restore the land to Elizabeth, Henry's widow, who had held the manor jointly with her husband. Eventually the lordship descended to their son Alan who had been born in 1343.

Alan died without issue, so on his death the manor devolved to Elizabeth, the daughter of John Martel of Cheverton, Somerset, who was married to Sir John Bonville. On Sir John's death in 1396 the land was inherited by his son William. It seems as if the county escheator had forgotten the orders of 1352, for in 1398, on the death of Bonville, he was again ordered to 'meddle no further with the manor of Great Glen' and to deliver it to Richard Stukley and Elizabeth his wife as John Bonville, at his death, had held the manor in the right of Elizabeth. In 1414 Elizabeth died leaving the manor to her son Roger Stukley. By 1422 Roger had died and his son Richard was Lord of the Manor. Richard died unmarried and the manor passed to Cecily Bonville, the wife of Thomas Grey, 1st Marquis of Dorset. From Cecily it passed to her grandson Henry who was created Duke of Suffolk in 1551. Three years later he was found guilty of treason and beheaded. After the duke's execution the manor was purchased by John Neale.

Population of Medieval Great Glen

With the absence of parish registers it is difficult to ascertain the population of any parish in the pre-Reformation period. However, between 1290 and 1434 there were fifty-eight lay subsidies which were levied to meet royal expenditure. Some of these records, which list names and the amount of tax levied, survive and give an insight both into the more well-to-do people of the parish and the wealth of the parish in general.

The 1327 subsidy for Glen lists twenty-six people who paid a total tax of sixty-five shillings, while five years later inflation put the parish levy up to eighty shillings This was the highest levy in the area with Burton Overy assessed at 49s 11d, Stretton Parva 28s, Newton Harcourt 16s and Wistow 30s. Although some family names are given, most people are given locative names such as Adam on the Hill, William on the Green, John de Foxton, Adam de Stretton and Richard de Tilton. One surname of especial interest in the 1332 subsidy is that of Alice Aleyn - a family name which is still to be found in the village today.

In 1347, to meet the expenses of Edward III's war against the Scots, a tax of one-twentieth of the value of all moveable goods was levied. Unfortunately the Great Glen returns for the infamous poll tax of 1381 are incomplete and give little idea of the make up of the village. However, what has survived show payments ranging from 6d (servants) to five shillings (Nicholas Walays, who was described as a franklin - a landowner of free but not noble birth).

By the mid-fifteenth century the village seems to have been in decline, for the 1445 subsidy of £4 2s was found to be too much and an abatement of nine shillings was made. By the 1524 subsidy family names had become common, some of which are still found in the area today, such as Glover, Ilif, Hodges, Linthwait and the ubiquitous Allens.[1]

---

1. *Lists of these lay subsidies giving lists of names and the amounts levied can be found in George Farnham's* Mediaeval Village Notes, *a copy of which is lodged in the Leicestershire Record Office.*

Chapter 2

Reformation to Restoration

The Dissolution of the Monasteries

In 1534 Henry VIII's struggles with the Church and the authority of Rome came to a head when he announced that he and not the Pope was the head of the Church of England. The following year Henry suppressed and confiscated the land of all religious houses with an income of less than £200 a year. This wealth did not satisfy the king and by March 1540 he had closed all the monasteries in the country. Some, such as Canterbury and Durham were converted into cathedrals while many others, Glen included, were sold to the laymen whose families had supported the religious institutions for generations. The vicar of Glen during these turbulent years was Thomas Thorpe, who had been installed in September 1493. Thorpe, a very adaptable man, was one of the few clergy who survived the ecclesiastical upheavals of the 1530s. He died in 1544 after faithfully serving the people of Glen for over fifty years.

Holders of Land

Prior to 1535 almost all the land in England was owned by either the Crown or the Church and with the Dissolution great changes were made in the distribution and ownership of land. In Great Glen records are scant but we know that in 1581 Queen Elizabeth leased several parcels of land, which had formally belonged to Owston Abbey, to Robert Cole for twenty-one years. The following year other land was leased to Henry Foxwell for an annual rent of £17 4s 9d. Others who leased Crown land in the Elizabethan years include William Langston who, with Elizabeth his wife and their son Robert, rented a tenement and half a virgate of land for £1 8s 4d a year. In 1553 Thomas Normandie rented a tenement, a croft and two oxgangs of land for a yearly payment of £1 6s 8d.

One of the main holders of land in the sixteenth and early seventeenth century was the Bale family of Saddington who had purchased the manor of Carlton Curlieu which had formerly

Sepulchral effigy of John Bale in the church of St Mary, Carlton Curlieu.

belonged to the Priory of Ulverscroft. In 1563 John Bale was in dispute with Thomas Linthwait over property in Glen which included a large house, two cottages and gardens, two orchards, eighty acres of land, thirty acres of meadow, forty acres of pasture, half an acre of wood and twenty acres of furze and heath.

Another of the major land holders at this time was the Hobson family which can be traced back to the Lay Subsidy of 1524 when Robert Hobson was assessed at six shillings, the fifth-highest levy in the parish. In 1578 Thomas was holding two messuages, one close of land and four virgates of land which had once belonged to Henry, Duke of Suffolk, who, as previously mentioned, had been executed for treason in 1554. The following year Robert, Thomas's heir, took out a twenty-one year lease for the property at forty-two shillings a year. The lease allowed Hobson housebote,[1] hedgebote, firebote, ploughbote and cartbote but only as long as he did not get over forty days in arrears with the rent. In 1600 he purchased the property outright for £110.

The Bothway family were in Glen by 1601 in which year William is mentioned in a deed as holding fourteen acres of arable land, two acres of meadow and ten acres of pasture. William was dead by 1605 but the Bothway family name was perpetuated and over a hundred years later part of Glen's land was still referred to as Bothways Close.

1. A 'bote' was a common right of taking timber from the waste of the manor for the repair of the subject in question.

The Linthwait family can also be traced back to the 1524 subsidy when Robert was assessed at 2s 6d. In 1633 William, son of Thomas, died aged thirty-eight leaving his eldest son Thomas a messuage, a cottage and two virgates of land, meadow and pasture and a piece of meadow called Prior's Round Hill. This may have got its name from the Prior family - in 1604 Thomas Prior died owning a messuage, one virgate of arable land and an undisclosed amount of meadow and pasture.

The Boultons can also be traced back to the Lay Subsidy of 1524 when Richard was assessed at 6s 6d - the third-highest levy in the village. In 1607 Robert Boulton left his nephew Lawrence a messuage and three and a half virgates of arable land, meadow and pasture. On Lawrence's death in 1632 he left some of his property to his brother Thomas and the rest to his wife Isabel, with the proviso that if she remarried she would only receive one-third of the land.

Possibly, with the exception of the lord of the manor, the richest family in the parish was the Hollyoaks. The first reference to the family in Glen is the 1593 birth of William to John, who died in 1615. In 1632 William married his second wife, Mary Chamberlain. He died two years later leaving his messuage, two cottages and five virgates of land meadow and pasture to his sixteen year old son Arthur who, in 1664 lived in the largest house in the village.

One of the seven richest men in the village mentioned in the Lay Subsidy of 1628 was Robert Green. The Greens were one of the oldest-established families in the village, as a William Green is mentioned in the Lay Subsidy of 1327.

In the 1628 subsidy was John Hurst. As well as a messuage, a virgate of arable land and meadow and pasture in Glen, Hurst also held a half-share in the manor of Fleckney which he had inherited in 1607. On his death in 1636 all the land passed to his son Thomas.

Descent of the Manor

The Neales became lord of the manor in 1553 when Thomas Gilbert sold the manorial rights to Sir Richard Neale, one of the Justices of the Common Pleas. From Richard the manor passed to his son Robert and so to his son John, who died in 1619. On

John's death his seventeen year old son George inherited the manor. An idea of the wealth of the family may be seen from the 1628 subsidy in which he was assessed at 32s - twice the amount levied on the other land holders in Glen. George died in 1634 without an heir and the manor passed to William Hewett of Dunton Bassett, who was married to Frances, daughter of Edward, George's half brother. William Hewett became High Sheriff of Leicestershire in 1647.

Civil War

During the 1630s the rising sense of power and growing self-consciousness of the gentry of both town and country became more marked as the rift between Crown and people widened. Conflict became inevitable and on 23 October 1642 the Battle of Edge Hill, Warwickshire, opened what we now know as the Civil War.

For over two years Glen was spared any part of the action. However, in June 1645 the people of the village received first-hand experience of the conflict. After the decisive Battle of Naseby, Northamptonshire, 14 June 1645, the defeated Royalists were pursued to Market Harborough and then along

Rupert's Rest, Main Street. Although built many years after Rupert's visit, the name reminds us of the tumultuous days of the 1640s.

what is now known as London Road as far as Great Glen, where the Cromwellians were checked by a small body of Royalist cavalry under the command of the Earl of Lichfield. On the following day the main Parliamentary army marched to Great Glen where they camped overnight before successfully attacking Leicester the next day (16 June). It is possible that some of the Parliamentarian army were quartered in the church and caused their customary wanton damage for, a few days later, Captain Richard Symonds, quartermaster in the royal army, visited the village and reported that all the church windows, bar one, were broken.

These were hectic times for the village, and for a few days it was at the centre of the war with men, horses and supplies from both sides coming and going through the village. The children would no doubt have been thrilled watching the Royalist army in full flight clattering though the village with the Cromwellians hard on their heels!

Prince Rupert, who led the royal cavalry at Naseby, is said to have spent the night before the battle in Great Glen. The house in question had a large room called Prince Rupert's Room and was demolished sometime before 1875. In 1836 a pistol and two rapiers of the time of Charles I were found in the roof of this house, which at the time was owned by one William Gilbert.

The house in Main Street which is now called Rupert's Rest post-dates the war and could not have been the house in question. It is more likely, however, that the prince stayed at arch-royalist Richard Halford's Wistow Hall rather than in a village whose lord of the manor, William Hewett, was sympathetic to Cromwell.

Halford, an ardent royalist, lived at Wistow Hall where he entertained Charles on his visits to the county. The last occasions when the King visited Wistow were the nights before and after the Battle of Naseby. Such was the hate felt towards Halford by the Parliamentarians that they repeatedly plundered Wistow Hall. As he owned much property in Glen many of his tenants may well have felt that they should share their landlord's support of the king and as such may have been hostile to the Parliamentarians. Halford died in 1658, two years before the Restoration of his beloved royal family.

During the flight from Naseby a boy saw a trooper throw a bag over a hedge. The lad retrieved it and took it to his employer, Thomas Hobson who, in spite of it being full of money, told the finder that it only contained nails. He kept it for himself and became a wealthy man. It is possible that a thief had taken advantage of the confusion after the battle and, being pursued, had thrown his loot away to avoid detection. Thomas Hobson is mentioned in a deed of 1670 as well as in glebe terriers of 1674, 1679, 1690 and 1698.

In September 1645, a few months after the Battle of Naseby, the vicar of Glen, Edward Cooper, died. Born in Glen in 1598 Cooper had studied at Trinity College, Oxford before being appointed to Glen in 1625. One of the richest men in the village in 1627 he married local girl Ann, daughter of Robert Hodges. Cooper's successor was Samuel Knightly who held the living until his death in 1690. In 1655 Knightley, a graduate of Corpus Christi College, Cambridge, helped the village collect 12s 4d for the Protestants of Piedmont who had survived an horrendous attack by a Catholic army.

Today in Great Glen there are five roads which remind us of the sanguine events of over 350 years ago: Cromwell Road, Naseby Way, Rupert Way, Edgehill Close and Halford Close.

The Hearth Tax

We can get an idea of the prosperity of Glen in the years just after the Restoration by studying the Hearth Tax Roll of 1664. Levied for the first time in 1662, with the intention of generating money for the 'better support of the king', every hearth and stove was taxed at 2s a year. Abolished in 1689, the surviving returns give an insight into which families lived in which types of houses and how prosperous they were. The 1664 roll for Glen, which raised a total of £5 2s, has survived and gives a picture of the parish in the postbellum years. Out of the forty-nine houses mentioned in the list the largest by far was that occupied by Arthur Hollyoak who had seven hearths. The vicarage, long since demolished, had three.[1]

---

1. *The Hearth Tax roll is transcribed in full in George Farnham's* Mediaeval Village Notes, *a copy of which is lodged in the Leicestershire Record Office.*

Chapter 3

The 18th and 19th Century Church

The Tower

The church had a spire until 1768 when, for safety reasons, it was taken down. The following year it was rebuilt by the Leicestershire architect John Wing, who seven years earlier had built the church of St John Baptist at nearby Kings Norton. The four master masons, Thomas Walton, John Thorpe, Thomas Thorpe and Robert Higgins, were each paid 2s 6d a day, and were assisted by three unnamed labourers who were each paid 1s 2d a day. Part of the work included three new belfry windows which were made at a total cost of £21. The final bill for the work came to £191 11s 1d, a sum which included £8 for the drawing of the plans.

There is a tradition that the tower was damaged by Cromwell's artillery in 1645 and this may well be the case. However, one reason for the tradition may stem from the tower being damaged by lightning one Sunday sometime between Archbishop Bonney's visitations of 1832 and 1836.[1]

The Condition of the Church

In 1776 Archdeacon James Bickman inspected the church and found it in such a filthy condition that he promptly ordered that the walls, which were thickly covered with plaster, were to be cleaned and whitewashed. He also ordered repairs to be made to the seats, the font cover, the east end of the north aisle, the north door and the porch.

Some of the work was done in 1780 when four men took three weeks to repair the roof and gutters at the cost of £27 17s 6d. This was exclusive of the 8s 4d expended on the required twenty ounces of nails. While John Barwell and John Weston of Carlton were being paid 12s 6d for repairing the east gable, other men

---

1. *Visitation reports are kept in the Leicestershire Record Office.*

were reflooring the uneven nave and Thomas Harrison was fencing the churchyard and putting in new gate posts.

Nine years later the church was still in a grubby state as when, in 1789, the local historian John Throsby visited Glen he was not over-impressed with what he saw. Vowing never to return, he noted that visitors to the church had to be careful that their clothes were not spoilt by the copious streams of water which ran down the mildewed walls. The seats still had not been repaired, for he observed that the nave was littered with broken benches 'richly adorned with the labour of spiders'. Throsby also observed that the local children were afraid of the church owing to the two 'monstrous figures of Time and Death staring like stuck pigs' which were painted, as were the Lord's Prayer and the Ten Commandments, on the nave wall. Throsby finished his remarks with the telling comment 'What a little Heaven is the church of Oadby, and what a . . . . is the church of Great Glen![1]

When Archbishop Andrew Burnaby visited the church in 1796 he ordered a gate be erected in the porch to keep out the cattle which were allowed to roam the churchyard. He further recommended that in future it should be grazed with sheep instead of cows and horses as the latter were apt to trample

St Cuthbert's church as it appeared in 1790.
(By kind permission of the Leicestershire Record Office)

1. John Throsby Select Views Vol. II page 319

down the graves and damage the headstones. The pews still had not been repaired.

In 1813 there was much controversy in the village when £783 1s 4d was borrowed to do more work on the church. Much to the disgust of the Wesleyans in the village the loan was paid back by a shilling levy on the church rate. This would not be known were it not for a note added onto the margin of the Poor Rate Returns for the years 1801-1817. The note reads 'Borrowed in 1813 the amount of the sum expended in repairing the church which was £783 1s 4d and it was unanimously agreed at a vestry to pay off the sum borrowed by a shilling levy every year which is the sum specified for the last four years under the church rate and constable's rate.'[1]

The porch, which as we have seen had needed attention almost forty years earlier, was found too decayed to be repaired and had to be demolished. A wood and plaster gallery, on which the choir stood to sing, accompanied by a bass viol, was erected at the west end and, at long last, new box-pews costing £786 were fitted. Although at the time they were described as 'very handsome', forty years later the Reverend Dodds referred to them as 'ignorant carpentry'. By 1832 the church was in as good a condition as it had been for many years, one observer going as far as to say that it was in an 'admirable state'.

The Clock

In 1796 Andrew Burnaby recommended that the sundial should be replaced with a clock which would 'remind the labouring poor of the hours of going to or returning from their labours'. It was not, however, for another fifty years before Charles Packe furnished the church with a clock that was fitted in the west face of the tower. Made by the renowned clock maker and jeweller Edward John Dent, the maker of the clock on the Houses of Parliament, St Cuthbert's new clock struck its first stroke on 13 November 1847. This new addition to the village was of great importance as now all the villagers could follow the same time, something that became even more important in 1854 when the railway came to the village. In 1873 Mr Goodacre was paid thirty shillings for attending to the clock, and in 1898 it was

1. *Leicestershire Record Office QS 92/2/65.*

repaired along with the tower. In 1940 the clock was repaired again, this time by J. Smith Ltd of Derby.

Henry Luke Dodds

Without a doubt the most controversial incumbent of St Cuthberts in the nineteenth century was Henry Luke Dodds. Born in 1811, in Woodford, Essex, Dodds studied at Christ Church College, Oxford. In 1838 he was ordained a deacon and appointed curate of Freshwater, Isle of Wight. Unmarried, he came to Glen in 1855 and immediately immersed himself in the work of the parish where he remained until his death on 10 May 1886. Dodds lived in the vicarage with his mother, Lucia, whose death in November 1878 affected him greatly. In the burial register, next to his mother's name, Dodds added *Eheu! Desideralissima*, 'Alas! What a loss!'

An orthodox and very learned divine, who expected everyone to be as committed to religion as he was, Dodds was, according to Mrs Packe, in all worldly matters a mere child. Indeed in 1869 she had occasion to write to her nephew, the Rev Charles William Packe, 'I might as well ask the advice of a child as apply to Mr Dodds on any matter of £sd'.[1]

An impulsive man who tried to do too much, whether anybody wanted it or not, it was not long before he commenced conducting a weekly Sunday service at Stretton Magna. As this was in addition to the two at Glen, he soon found that the three services were too much and so provided a curate. However he soon found that this was costing him too much and, without due thought or consideration as to the consequences, cancelled the Stretton services. A very conservative man, he was still writing with a quill pen in 1886, he found it hard to see any point of view but his own and caused a lot of ill-feeling in the parish by his ingrained and open hatred of dissenters.

In 1859 Dodds presented to the church a two-handled urn-shaped loving cup, which had been made, in 1795, by Lambert and Rawlings, gold and silversmiths of Coventry Street, London. The cup's cover was surmounted with a figure of St Cuthbert

---

1. *The Leicestershire Record Office holds many letters which were passed between the Packe family and Dodds. It is from these, DE849/23/1-58 that most of the contents of this chapter have been obtained.*

holding his pastoral staff in his left hand with the head of King Oswald in his right. Inscribed 'This cup was given by the Reverend Henry Luke Dodds to the church in Great Glen to be used for the loving cup at the Feast of the Dedication AD1859', the intention was that the cup should be used every year at the feast which followed the thanksgiving service on the Sunday nearest 22 November.

Dodds had not been in the parish long before his eccentricity began to bring him into constant friction with Charles William Packe of Prestwold who had purchased the manor of Great Glen in 1839. In August 1868 Dodds told Packe that, 'due to a secret duty imposed upon himself', he intended to resign as from 1 May 1869. This news was greeted with delight by the Packe family who lost no time in trying to obtain someone to replace him and restore harmony in the parish.

Although the resignation was supposed to have been kept secret, the news leaked out and in December it became known that the bishop, for reasons not clear, had refused to accept Dodds' resignation. It is possible that the bishop's decision was based on representations from Dodds' friends in the parish who a few weeks earlier had requested him to remain in Glen 'as his Christian kindness and attention to his parishioners have secured their universal goodwill and respect'. In any event the result was that the Packes still had a 'somewhat awkward and inefficient person' as their clergyman for a time longer. Mrs Packe was at a loss to know why the resignation had not been accepted as, in her view, it would have been better for the parish if it had.

Packe, who considered the situation 'very vexatious' if not 'an insuperable calamity', commented that it was to melt and not to burn that coals of fire were heaped on his enemy's head, and went on to observe it seemed an ideal opportunity of making a good fire. In the event Dodds served the parish for another eighteen years.

Nineteenth Century Church Restoration

In March 1862 Dodds first mooted his idea of restoring St Cuthbert's. When he mentioned his plan to his patron, Packe thought that he was being asked to pay for the work himself and told Dodds in no uncertain terms that he had more pressing things on which to spend his money. He went on to say that he had many calls upon his funds for works of piety and charity and, although he accepted Dodds' feelings on the subject, reluctantly he put the fabric of St Cuthbert's near the bottom of his list. He also turned down the vicar's suggestion of raising a church rate for the proposed restoration and advised Dodds to see if there was an endowment fund which could be used for such a purpose and in the meantime not to tell anyone else of his idea.

The matter seems to have been put on the back burner for three years, until December 1865, when, at a lively meeting of the Society for the Propagation of the Gospel, Dodds started a church restoration fund. Over the next few years there were various fund raising events, such as concerts and sales of work were held, but the money came in very slowly and were it not for the change in attitude and generosity of Charles Packe, it would have been many years before the work, which cost about £3,000, could be done. In April 1875 the vestry approved the restoration work, which commenced the following June. The London firm of architects Carpenter & Ingelow and the Kibworth builder John Loveday were engaged with Mr Lucas as the clerk of the works.

Using Mountsorrel granite and Ancaster stone, the work included a new parapet to the tower, new chancel, chancel arch, vestry, south wall to nave and a south porch to replace that taken down in 1813. The nave was re-roofed on the original pitch and the false floor, laid a hundred years earlier almost two feet above the original level, was taken up, revealing the hitherto hidden bases of the columns. Although the intention was that all the sepulchral slabs were to be replaced in their original position, with those that were hidden under the new floor marked by brass plates set into the floor above the slabs, this was not done and many were used to pave the ground floor of the tower under the belfry. The brass plates never were installed.

The windows regained their tracery and mullions; the Romanesque font was replaced and a new base with five steps was made for the altar, which was furnished by a cross. The base of the new brass eagle lectern, made by Potter of London and purchased by subscription, was inscribed with the names of the donors. The needs of the body were not forgotten as Mr Johnson of Leicester installed a new heating system.

Part of the work involved the demolition of the west end gallery and box-pews which had been built in 1813. With the new seating Dodds took the opportunity of abolishing the system of appropriated seats, whereby the more well-to-do paid an annual rent for the best pews while the poor had to make do with what was left. Previously out of the 322 available seats as many as 224 were appropriated leaving only 98 for those who could not afford to pay. One of the pew renters was Arthur Haymes who rented three - one for his family and two for his servants. Not all the old wood was thrown away, some was recycled and made into the candelabras which replaced the hitherto unsightly candle holders.

In August 1876 Dodds asked the bishop's chaplain if he thought the church would need reconsecrating before it was re-opened after the restoration. When Packe found out what his vicar had done he got very angry telling Dodds that he hoped he had not mentioned his name in the request! Dodds replied that he felt everyone had a right to ask advice of the bishop and that he did not need permission from anybody before he did. Although the bishop, William Connor, felt that there had not been enough rebuilding to warrant a reconsecration, he did grace the re-opening ceremony.

A few weeks before the re-opening Dodds complained to Packe that the sexton, William Allen, had not only wheeled

The nave as it looked in 1874. Note the box-pews and the position of the font. Compare this with illustration opposite. (By kind permission of Rev J. Wellington.)

away the surplus soil, which had been taken out of the church when the heating apparatus was installed in August 1876 and left piled up outside the church, but he had also, on the indirect instruction of Packe, cut down the hedge which separated the old from the new churchyards. Dodds went on to question whether Packe had a legal right to order the removal of the churchyard fence without the consent of the incumbent. This was just too much for Packe, a qualified lawyer, who replied by not only calling into question Dodds' behaviour as a clergyman, but also accused him of doing his best to introduce discord into the parish when, with the re-opening of the church only weeks away, he should have been insuring that everyone was pulling together to promote harmony in the village. Packe went on to remind Dodds that even though he had refused to co-operate with the building committee, leaving them with all the responsibility, both he and Hodgkin Lewin, churchwarden, had always consulted him, even on minor matters.

As to the removal of the soil Packe, who by now was at the end of his tether, testily asked 'Surely you do not pretend that the work of wheeling out all that earth, which had been going on for a few weeks, was done without your knowledge and sanction. If I did not mention it, it was because it was right before your eyes'.

On 30 November 1876 the church was re-opened with a collection of £97. As thanks for his efforts on behalf of the church, some of Dodds' friends took the opport-unity of presenting him with a silver cup, a vessel which is still kept in the vestry. The

The nave after restoration in 1876. Compare this with illustration opposite. (By kind permission of Rev J. Wellington.)

25

following day St Helen's church at Gumley, which had also been restored, was re-opened. Indeed, the second half of the nineteenth century was a period of church restoration all over the country. In 1866 it had been the turn of St Andrew's, Burton Overy, and, four years later in 1880, St Mary's, Carlton Curlieu.

Note left by Henry Dodds for his successor. Written with a quill pen, it reads 'The churchyard is the vicar's freehold. When I came here the vicar received £4 a year rent for it. I reduced it to £3. After some years I gave the grass of the churchyard sometimes to the clerk and sometimes to other persons - it is desirable that the clerk should not suppose that he has a right to it. The church is very weak in the parish. The quiet but very vigorous opposition to it is led by the Haycocks and Mrs Cooper. The Clements are dissenters though they come to church. The church people have little zeal especially for missions.'
(By permission of the Leicestershire Record Office.)

Chapter 4

The Land

Open Fields

Up until the mid-nineteenth century most people worked on the land. Even those who had other occupations, such as the blacksmith and the miller had their own strips in the common fields because almost everyone was self-sufficient, growing their own food.

Before the enclosures of 1759 and 1760 the land in Great Glen was farmed on the open field system whereby each man had his own share of the parish land. The emergence of this two or three field system took place at a time before documentary evidence survives so we do know exactly when it started. Some historians believe that the fields were an extension of the Roman *vill* while others contend that they were an Anglo-Saxon innovation. In any event, it is certain that the fields were in existence by the time the Normans reached the Midlands in the mid-eleventh century.

The reasons for this method of cultivation are also clouded in the mists of time. However, it is likely that the strip system originated at a period when no one man had a full ox team, a circumstance necess-itating several men having to contribute their animal to make the team.

Reconstruction of the pre-enclosure open fields of Great Glen.

So that no one man would have all the good land, originally each man would have had strips, or furlongs, in various parts of the fields. The strips were allotted in rotation so newcomers to the village did not take any of the existing villagers' land as his strips became, by a natural process, intermixed with those of the others. There were no physical partitions between each man's land, only a stake or large stone at the corners marked one holding from another. Apart from some medieval boundaries, such as the one between Glen's Middle and Road Fields, there were few hedges and the open land stretched as far as the eye could see.

Each bundle of strips, which varied in size according to the nature of the soil and the lie of the land, made up the furlongs, which were separated from one another by grass balks. The furlongs, originally 220 by 22 yards, that is a day's ploughing for one team, in their turn were grouped together into two or three compact fields of roughly equal size.

Great Glen is unusual inasmuch that there were two sets of open fields - the Upper, or North End Fields and the Nether, or South End Fields. The reasons for this may be due to the village having two central points - one in the present Orchard Lane area and the other to the east of the church. As early as 1279 the land which composed the parish was part of two lordships; eleven ploughlands were held by Robert Martell, lord of the manor, while the rest was held by his neighbour, Richard Harcourt.

Ridge and Furrow

Before enclosure the land in the open fields was cultivated on the ridge and furrow principle. Evidence of this can be seen in many parts of Glen where the ridges have been fossilised under grass, in some cases for many centuries. The ridges and furrows in the fields, which represent the pattern of agriculture at the time that it was last ploughed, remind us that at one time this was arable land which at some point was given over to pasture. The two main possible reasons for this are either the introduction of sheep farming or as a sign that there was a reduction in the labour force in the village - usually because of plague in the fourteenth century. That Glen suffered from depopulation we know from the internal evidence of the lay subsidy of 1445 which shows that the village's assessment of tax of £4 2*s* was abated by nine shillings.

The ridges and furrows take us back to the days when farmers considered what crops were needed for their family's and cattle's consumption and not, as is the case today, what crops would sell. It was a time before artificial fertilisers when three-year rotation was practised in which the first year saw wheat or rye for bread, the second year beans and barley for livestock and beer, and the third year left fallow and used as pasture for cattle, whose manure fed the land for the next crop. After the crops were lifted the land was put over to common pasture for a month or so before the next crop was sown. This method of farming meant, of course, that each man had to sow and harvest the same crop at the same time as his neighbour.

Good ploughing was the foundation of all cultivation and ploughmen took great pride in their work. Ploughing the first furrow always required great skill in steering the team towards a distant point without the slightest deviation or looking backwards. Thereafter one horse walked in the furrow and the other on the unploughed land.

Enclosure

Although various small 'closes', what we today would term fields, had been created by the mid-eighteenth century, most of the open fields of Great Glen were enclosed by two Acts of Parliament in 1759 and 1760. We get an idea of some of these early enclosures from glebe terriers (which record details of fields and rents paid), which in the case of Great Glen survive from the mid-seventeenth century, and from wills. For instance, from a glebe terrier of 1698 we learn that there were three cow pastures in the north end and twenty sheep commons in the south end of Mill Field - the area between the present Oaks and London Roads.

The enclosure movement of the eighteenth century was concerned with the removal of the traditional open or common fields and their replacement with the enclosed fields which are part of our familiar landscape today. This change in land usage had various effects on the parish, the most visual being the new squarish fields laid out by the commissioners. These fields had to be surrounded by a hedge, in which the gates and stiles were

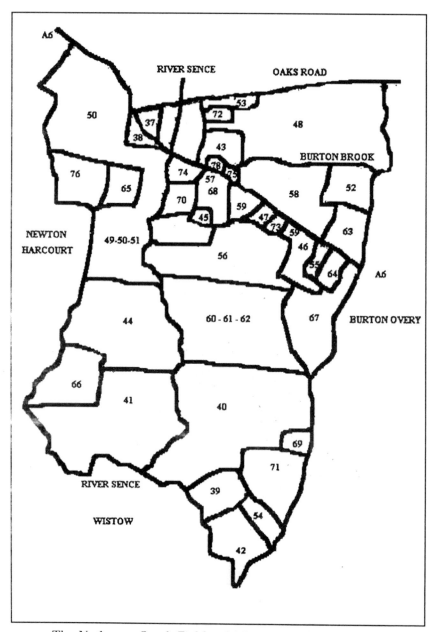

The Nether or South Fields which were enclosed in 1760

fitted which communicated with the roads and public footpaths which are a part of the landscape today.

Enclosure was not cheap for the total legal cost for Great Glen amounted to no less than £1,215 6s 6d. This included the cost of parliamentary legislation and the expenses of the commissioners who drew up the awards.

This new system of land tenure also brought about a change in the layout of the village. Before enclosure almost everybody lived in the centre of the village. However, now that the farmers had their own land they built isolated red brick farmhouses set in their own fields. Example of these can be seen in various parts of the village. These new farms were usually set out on a line with the old furlongs.

Framework Knitting

One of the indirect changes brought about by Enclosure included the establishment of framework knitting as a major cottage industry in the village. This came about as people who previously had rights on the common fields became totally or partly dispossessed. The first recorded mention of framework knitting in Great Glen is in 1722 when Richard Pinder's daughter Mary married Thomas Wright, a framework knitter of Fleckney. Knitting was popular as it could be done in the home and made work available for all members of the family, especially women.

By 1777 the industry had become firmly established in Glen with

---

Opposite page: *The Nether, or South End Fields enclosed in 1760. The numbers refer to the allocation of land.*

37–38: The Vicar	66: Thomas Franks
39–40: William Hewett	67–69: William King, Isaiah King
41–43: William Halford	and John Franks
44–48: William Hewett	70: John Day
49–55: George Cooper	71: James Bell
56–57: William Young	72: Matthew Harrison
58–59: Green Hodgkin	73: John Chamberlain
60–62: John Foster	74: Thomas Terry
63: Charles Faulkner	75: Thomas Blackwell and
64: William Darker	Dorothy Campion
65: William Simpson	76: Town Land (between 75 & 58)

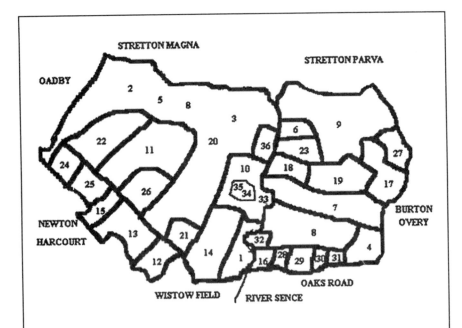

1: The Vicar (Caleb Robinson)
2 - 6: William Hewett
7: Peter Shuter
8 - 9: Green Hodgkin
10 - 11: Rober Haymes
12: George Cooper
13: Christian Cooper
14 - 15: Thomas Hobson
16 - 17: Thomas Linthwaite
18: John Linthwaite
19 - 20: Thomas Goodrich
21: Mary Hutchins
22: Thomas Plummer

23: Thomas Franks
24: Mary Wilkins
25: Richard Eltrington
26: John Day
27: William Palmer
28: Joseph Bull
29: Thomas Hilton
30: William Darker
31: John Goodacre
32 - 33: David Grant
34: William King
35: William Simpson
36: James Wright

The Upper, or North End Fields, enclosed in 1759.
The numbers refer to the allocation of land.

frames being held by many people including John Pywell, Joseph Ellingworth, Thomas Vann, John Collins and Edward Jee. Even the blacksmith, Robert Chamberlain had a frame. Framework knitting became widespread in Great Glen in the early nineteenth century.

Peep Row

In 1840 a terrace of ten cottages in Main Street, known as Peep Row, was built for framework knitters. The houses, which featured large chimneys and hoodmoulded diagonally-glazed windows, were financed by Charles Packe who fitted the dwellings with every necessary convenience which 'might render them a comfortable asylum for persons customarily considered to be superior of that class of persons for whose residence they are designed'. Let out at rents so low and moderate 'as to make them a grateful charity to those who may be allowed to obtain them' the houses were a beneficial addition to the village.

Caleb Robinson

Another of the changes caused by enclosure was the way that the vicar was paid. Up until this time he, and his predecessors, had been paid tithes at various times of the year. Now, however, the new landowners were to pay him an annual lump sum of £32. The vicar at the time of enclosure was Caleb Robinson.

Behind the old blacksmith's shop in High Street stands this seventeenth century cruck timber-framed house. At the time of enclosure, in 1760, the house was occupied by Ralph and Mary Bull.

Born at Billesdon in 1706 Caleb's father Richard sent his son to Oakham School and then to St John's College, Cambridge. Appointed curate of Arthingworth, just over the Northamptonshire border, in 1731 Caleb was given the living of Bisbrook, Rutland, before being appointed Rector of Great Glen in 1745, a post he held till his death in 1770. Caleb Robinson was buried in Billesdon churchyard where a headstone still stands to his memory.

Apparently there was an epidemic in the village in 1754. There are entries in the parish register concerning the protectionist Burials in Woollen Acts of 1666 and 1678. These Acts ordered that all corpses had to be buried in wool and also that the coffin had to be lined in the same material. Within eight days of a burial an affidavit had to be made that the law had been complied with. The fine for non-compliance with the law was five pounds. However, as half of this was given to the informant, many people who wished their kin to be buried in other materials informed on themselves thereby having only to pay half the mandatory fine. The law was finally repealed in 1814. In 1754 there are entries in the Glen register stating that affadavits were omitted because the neighbouring clergy "dusst not admitt to take them, as they were afraid that the persons deceased might have died of some infectious distemper".

The 1760s were an eventful decade in Glen. On 19 January 1761 William Simpson's wife, Mary, was delivered of a baby girl. The infant must have been very ill for, fearing that the vicar would not arrive in time, the midwife, using her ecclesiastical right, baptised the child herself. However, no doubt due to the stressful circumstances, she mistakenly christened the baby girl William. 'William' died soon after and was buried two days later.

In April 1764, local man Robert Day was arrested for stealing two sheep, the property of George Cooper. At the July assizes he was sentenced to 14 years transportation to Virginia. Almost two years to the day of his arrest, 11 April 1766, his wife, Ann, gave birth to a daughter, Elizabeth. In the baptism register Robinson morally remarked that Ann was the wife of Robert Day 'who, about two years ago, was transported to His Majesties Plantations abroad'.

Another event concerned the 'witches'. In June 1760 two unnamed old women of Glen fell out and in the height of their argument vehemently accused each other of witchcraft. They both agreed to be dipped by way of trial and, after being stripped to their petticoats, with their thumbs and great toes tied together and a thick rope tied about their waists, they were thown into a pool of water. One immediately sunk - an indication that she was innocent. The other woman, however, struggled for a short time on the surface - an infallible sign of being a witch! They were both pulled out and the 'guilty' party made to impeach her fellow witches. With tongue in cheek she told her tormentors that there were several old women at Burton Overy who were as much witches as she was.

This was enough for the 'witchfinders' who immediately proceeded to Burton where they made another poor old woman undergo the same water treatment, but as there was no unanimous verdict she was left by the side of the pool to make her own way home. The next day two other suspects in Burton were forced to undergo the same aquatic ordeal. Thankfully justice prevailed and at the next Assize two of the ringleaders were sentenced to a day in the pillory followed by one month imprisonment. Twenty others who took part in the disgraceful affair were each fined.

Fox-hunting

Houses at the top end of High Street have such rural names as Ford View House, Field Edge, and Paddock Cottage, while just past the Royal Oak is a row of nineteenth century cottages which still have the entrances through which coaches and carts would pass into the yards behind. Nearby Console Cottages were built by Thomas Crick in 1874.

On Oaks Road, just before the sharp left turn, where the bridleway shows the route of the original road, is Glen Oaks, a spinney which in the nineteenth century was planted as a fox cover, to benefit the barbaric pastime of fox hunting - the spinney being an area where foxes were encouraged to breed so that the 'unspeakable could pursue the uneatable'!

Flooding

In the nineteenth century Oaks Road, or Burton Lane as it was then called, was liable to flooding. In 1882, after a bigger than usual deluge, concern was expressed about the bad state of the water. It was claimed that before the flood there had been no complaints or illness caused by the water but now the wells had to be cleaned out as sewage from the houses in the road had been washed into the wells.

The River Sence gets its name from the Old English word *sence* which means 'cup' - signifying a copious flow of water. It begins life as the Coplow Brook on Life Hill, near Billesdon, and flows into the Soar in the vicinity of Enderby Bridge by Jubilee Park on the B582. Until the 1930s, the river in Church Road was crossed by a ford which, in the nineteenth century, according to William Bithrey, a piano tuner from Leicester who often visited Great Glen in the course of his work, was often impassable 'without the risk of being drowned'.

In spite of the vestry presenting a memorial to the county magistrates in 1874 showing the necessity of bridging the ford, nothing was done and so, three years later, the village elders felt compelled to bring the matter to the attention of the sanitary authorities. A few months later a committee was formed and nearly £100 raised for cleaning out the brook. This

Oaks Road, formerly called Burton Lane.

work was never carried out and, in October 1880, there were once again disastrous floods in the village with great loss of property. The women and children had to go to higher ground for safety while the men had to wade to work. The ford was finally bridged in 1927. In May 1932, the attendance at the chapel Sunday school anniversary was affected by the another flood which made the roads leading to the village impassable until the late afternoon.

Great Glen's Methodist chapel was built in 1827. Most of the leading artisan families of the village were dissenters including William Edgley, miller; Thomas Batchelor, bricklayer; Daniel Allen, blacksmith; Solomon Banks, watchmaker; Joseph Smeeton, framework knitter; Thomas Smeeton, carpenter; John Hawley, grocer; John Haycock, builder; Robert Holyoak, tailor; Robert Scampton, carpenter; and William Scott, tailor. The Sunday School building was added some fifty years later, while the connecting hall was built in 1991.

Chapter 5

The Relief of the Poor

> *Theirs is yon house that holds the parish poor*
> *Whose walls of mud scarce bear the broken door;*
> *There, where the putrid vapours flagging, play,*
> *And the dull wheel hums doleful through the day.*

George Crabb *The Poor House*

Elizabethan Poor Law

Although the duty for relieving the poor in the medieval period was legally incumbent upon the manor, it was generally recognised as falling morally upon the church. In 1572 a new poor law was passed which put the responsibility for maintaining the poor on the parish in which they lived. Those responsible for seeing this law carried out were the overseers of the poor who were annually selected from the churchwardens and the substantial householders of the parish. As the cost of supporting the poor was funded by taxing the parishioners much care was taken to ensure that only genuine parishioners were helped.

The records of the names of many of Glen's early overseers have been lost and the first that we know about are Thomas Hobson and William Allen. These two men are mentioned on a bond of 1693 in which John Greene, butcher of Great Glen, and William Pebody, dyer of Huncote, paid £30 to the overseers to save the parish from any expense to which it might become liable by reason of John Collingwood, a labourer and his family of Illston on the Hill, settling in the parish. This was to ensure that if Collingwood became unable to work the parish inhabitants would not have to support him.

The Workhouse

In 1722–23 an Act of Parliament was passed which enabled the overseers and churchwardens, with the consent of the majority of the inhabitants of the parish, to purchase or hire buildings for maintaining and employing the poor. The first surviving reference to a workhouse in Glen is dated February 1749 when the turnpike trustees' minutes record that the footpath from the town houses, on the present London Road, to Mr Cooper's house, on the site of The Yews, was repaired.

About 1785 a new workhouse was built on the corner of the present Station Lane and the road to Newton Harcourt. The building was originally thatched as the accounts tell us that in November 1811 Thomas Rowe and William Bird were each paid three shillings and twopence a day for thatching the house, work which took them twelve days. At the same time the workhouse yard was covered with 'riddlings', the small stones which fell through the riddle or coarse sieve.

The workhouse was self-sufficient with its own farm to provide the inmates with food as well as hay and straw. In 1813 this field was fenced by Richard Wormell who received eight shillings and sixpence for his labour. The house also had its own cow, a new one being purchased in 1813 for £16 19s. Some of the inhabitants worked as framework knitters on one of the two frames which Robert Nosely leased to the house for two shillings a week.

Workhouse records are rather patchy but those for 1802–3 have survived and tell us that in that year the house relieved fourteen persons as well as an additional forty-eight adults and forty-three children who received outdoor relief. In the same period 427 passing vagabonds were given a few pence to enable them to carry on to the next parish. The road from Leicester to Kibworth seems to have been full of vagrants and vagabonds for in March 1807 it was felt necessary to order that all persons 'lodging in or under tents carriages or any other thing placed upon the side of the road' would be arrested and proceeded against as vagrants.

In the early nineteenth century it was mandatory for each parish to supply two or three men for the county militia. Chosen by ballot, the drawn men had to serve unless they could obtain substitutes, usually for a fee of £5 or £10. Obviously the poorer section of the community could not afford to buy substitutes and so, during their tour of duty, the parish would pay for the upkeep of their families. One such case in Great Glen was in

May 1813, when the overseers paid *2s 2d* to the families of John Nosley, James Elingworth, Edward Burdett and William Burdett who were serving in the militia.

Poor Law Apprenticeships

As apprenticeship gave legal settlement they were one way in which parish overseers could palm off their pauper children in someone else's parish. Sixty-seven apprenticeship indentures for young people bound as apprentices by the parish of Great Glen survive from between 1737 and 1835. Fifty-four of the children were apprenticed to masters outside the parish. During the period of apprenticeship, usually seven years, the master provided board and lodging and, at the end of the period the young people were given two suits of clothes - one for weekdays and one for Sundays. The apprentice in return, among other things, had to promise not to 'commit fornication nor contract matrimony within the said term'. He was also instructed not to play at cards, dice, tables, or any other unlawful games.

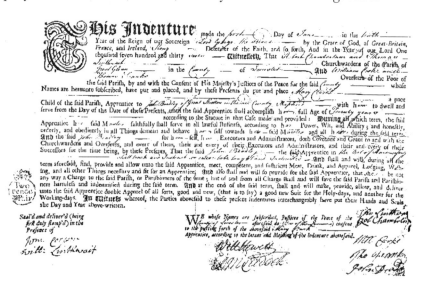

An apprenticeship indenture dated 1 June 1737 binding Mary Clark 'a poor child of this parish' to John Bradley, shepherd, of Stretton Magna who was to instruct Mary in 'the art of housewifery'.
(By permission of the Leicestershire Record Office)

The twelve girls for whom indentures survive were all to learn 'the art and mastery of housewifery' - in other words they were house servants. Of the fifty-five boys, thirty-five were apprenticed to framework knitters (all pre-1825 indentures are to framework knitters); nine to cordwainers (shoemakers); three to tailors; two each to hairdressers, framesmiths and carpenters; and one each to a woolcomber and sinker maker.

Bastardy Bonds

Bastardy bonds were a means of insuring a parish against the cost of maintaining children born to single mothers. Fathers, when known, were made responsible for the upkeep of their child by a lump sum paid to the parish in discharge of all responsiblility or by a bond which indemnified the parish from financial liability.

One such bond which has survived, dated 10 December 1784, concerns Mary Falkner, a single woman, who gave birth on 30 November 1784 to a son, George, who had been fathered by Otho Wigginton. Otho's father, Francis, a butcher of Manton, Rutland, gave the Great Glen churchwardens (John Day and John Linthwaite) and the overseers of the poor (David Grant and Isaiah King) a bond of forty pounds which indemnified the parish from 'all manner of taxes, rates, assessments and charges whatsoever for and by reason of the birth, education and maintainence of the said child'.

Settlement and Removal Orders

By the eighteenth century Great Glen, like any other parish, had to control the influx of labour. If a stranger settled in the parish he was liable to be removed forthwith unless he gained a legal settlement by renting a tenement of £10 or found security to discharge the parish in the event of illness or unemployment. It was not unknown for a parish to take legal action to prevent or argue settlement even though the legal fees far outweighed the cost of keeping the person in the parish!

Between July 1831 and April 1834 Great Glen and Leire were in contention over the settlement of one Mary Stevens and her three children - Ann, Catherine and Thomas. Mary's late husband had been a tenant of a house in Leire at a rent of £3 a year and after his death Mary continued paying the rent thereby keeping her legal settlement at Leire. However, Leire claimed that this was not so as the tenancy had been changed from a monthly to a weekly one. In the event Glen won the case and Mary was allowed to remain in Leire. The legal costs, which were awarded against Leire, came to a massive £94 16s 4d.

To rid a parish of a person who had no legal settlement the parish had to get a removal order. In December 1820 the Glen churchwardens and overseers of the poor complained that John Payne had come to inhabit the parish without a legal settlement. Not wanting Payne to become chargeable to Glen the overseers took legal action and Payne was ordered to be removed to Uppingham, his last place of legal settlement.

In May 1824 the parish of St Margaret's, Leicester, ordered that John Coulson, his wife Ann, and their three children William (7), James (5) and John (18 months) be removed to Glen. The court's opinion was that as Coulson did not have a legal settlement in St Margaret's he should be removed back to his last place of settlement. It was, however, soon discovered that the family had never been to Glen and so the order was rescinded and the removal abandoned.

Route Passes

In June 1836 Thomas Hobson, Glen's overseer of the poor, was reimbursed £12 3s 1d by the County Treasurer in lieu of payments he had made to twenty-six discharged prisoners. These men would have been in possession of route passes which gave them the means to return to their last place of legal settlement. On production of the pass to the overseers of the parishes though which they passed the men were paid up to 1½d per mile to cover their expenses to the next place on the pass. When the discharged prisoner got home the pass was given up to the overseer who returned it to the prison from whence the prisoner came. The overseers were then repaid by the county treasurer.

Town Land (or Poor Land) Charity

The earliest surviving deed concerning this charity is dated 18 October 1666. In it William Hobson conveyed a yardland (about 30 acres) to eighteen trustees including Neal Hewett, the lord of

The Yews. This may be on the site of the original manor house. The present house was built in the late eighteenth century for George Cooper, one of the village's major land owners.

the manor. The rents from the land were used for repairing the church, the highways and bridges as well as for the relief of the poor.

On enclosure in 1760 sixteen acres were endowed to the charity, fifteen in Wistow Field (on the road from Glen to Newton) and one in the East Field. In 1838 the land was held by Thomas Innocent, a miller, who had the land rent free as compensation for his providing water for the parish pit in Wash Pit Close. The Wistow Field land, which was pasture, was divided into three closes (Great Close, 7 acres; Top Close, 4 acres and House Close, 4 acres) and let every year to the highest bidder at an auction held at the Easter meeting of the vestry. In 1853 the charity's income of £45 18s 2d was spent on repairing the church (£17 2s 1d); repairing bridges (£4 15s 6d) causeways and highways (£7 7s 9d); relief of the poor (£9 9s 6d).

In 1876 Henry Dodds gave two £100 Portuguese bonds and the sum of £42 9s 2d cash which was invested in land. Two-thirds of the income went to the church choir (the Singers' Field) and the other third to newly-married poor persons who lived in the parish and regularly attended church, on the birth of their first child.

A few months later these two charities merged to form St Cuthbert's Money. This fund was put in the care of three trustees - the incumbent of the day, George Pick and Thomas Capell (parish clerk). One-third was for the maintenance and repair of the parish church (with the exception of the chancel) and providing insurance against fire; one-third for maintaining and keeping in good repair the bridges, causeways and highways and the other third towards providing water and drainage. The annual income was accumulated and invested until the principal reached £500 when it was used to purchase a piece of land which was called St Cuthbert's Land.

By 1896 the endowment consisted of a two acre field which was let out at a yearly rent of £7; £50 in New Consols and £37 6s 5d cash in the Leicester Savings Bank.

Poor Law Reform of 1834

The Poor Law was reformed in 1834 with the amalgamation of parishes into Poor Law Unions with one central workhouse. Although a distinction was made between those who could not and those who would not work, relief in the workhouse was to be as unattractive as possible, and only to be considered as the last resort. The well-to-do arrogantly propounded, as many still do today, that people were poor because they were lazy. The threat of the workhouse, they naïvely believed, would make them buck up their ideas. In the house there was a rigid classification with separation of able-bodied men; able-bodied women; children (who were to be educated by qualified schoolmasters); and the elderly, who were to be allowed to 'enjoy their indulgences'.

The men and women had their own day room with stairs leading to the dormitories, which were furnished with canvas-covered iron bedsteads, which had cost twenty-seven shillings and sixpence each.

In some cases where the parents could not maintain their own children the youngsters were removed from their families and taken to the workhouse. In June 1839, two of George Grain's daughters suffered this fate, and in February 1841, George Green, who had a wife and six children, had his relief reduced to three shillings a week and his ten year old daughter, Mary, taken into the care of the house. In February 1841 two of William Grain's eight children, Mary and Catherine, were taken to the house as was John Burdette's fourteen week-old son.

In 1835 the pay of the workhouse master, John Grain, rose from six shillings to nine shillings and sixpence a week. This rise, however, did not prevent him from resigning at the end of that year. In 1836 Great Glen workhouse, 'a small inconvenient building' which could hold between seventy and eighty inmates, was taken over by the newly-created Billeston Poor Law Union. The Union rented it from the parish for £30 a year, but in January 1837, it was reduced to £20.

The building was obviously in need of attention for, in the spring of 1836, local men William Horton, Thomas Batchelor and Samuel Bettoney were engaged to repair the walls and windows while John Glover brought in new furniture. By 1839 the old thatched roof had been tiled, for in January of that year it was reported that slates and ridge tiles had been blown off in a gale. In May 1840 the walls of the house were made higher, thereby giving 'more security with greater separation of the wards'.

The first Union workhouse master was Mr Finney whose salary of £7 a year was augmented by free board and lodging and an allowance of £1 a quarter for ale. Finney's work was not to the satisfaction of the Union for in January 1837 part of his claim for expenses was refused and the Union wrote to the Poor Law Commissioners with the request that Finney be dismissed. The letter went on to suggest that the workhouse should be closed and arrangements made with a neighbouring parish for the use of their workhouse at so much a head. This request was denied.

The following June, Finney, who was heading towards a nervous breakdown, complained about the behavior of Samuel Bull, one of the inmates, whom Finney alleged had threated his life. However, on examination by the magistrate, Isaac Hodgson JP, the master was unable to substantiate any of his accusations. Towards the end of the interview Finney broke down, becoming verbally abusive towards Hodgson. He finally asked if he could retire, a request which was immediately granted. Out of the seven applicants for the post, which was advertised in the *Leicester Journal* and *Leicester Chronicle*, Benjamin and Ann Dean of Leicester were appointed.

In June 1840 Henry Corrance, curate of Great Glen applied to the board of the Union for some remuneration for his work at the workhouse. The board, however, considered that as the master and matron read morning and evening prayers, along with the fact that the inmates attended public worship at the church every Sunday, they did not feel disposed to appoint a chaplain. They did, however, express the hope that Corrance would not discontinue his attentions at the workhouse on any pecuniary motives.

The house was kept clean and the inmates vaccinated on admission to keep them healthy. The aged and infirm, who were left to their own devices, were provided with books, including a Bible and six prayer books, by the Society for the Promotion of Christian Knowledge at a cost of £3 14s 5d.

Food was supplied by the local traders who contracted with the union to sell commodities at set prices. In July 1838 the contract for groceries was given to Mr Webster who offered black tea at 5s a pound, raw sugar at 7d a pound, rice at 2½d a pound, brown soap 5½d a pound and candles at 6s 6d a dozen. In May 1839 Samuel Eaton was contracted to supply shoes for the workhouse. As well as normal meals throughout the year Christmas was special as the inmates were allowed roast beef, plum pudding and ale - a quart for men and a pint for women and children.

Occupation in the Workhouse

As at any one time there were only a few children in the house the Union did not see the need to appoint a teacher. To save on expense the children, whose schoolroom was over the female day room, were taught by one of the adult paupers. The older girls, when work was available, were usually employed in sewing. Some of the more able-bodied inmates worked in the garden under the watchful eye of William Larkin who, in 1836, was being paid seven shillings a week. As well as growing food for the inmates the garden also produced a surplus which was sold in aid of Union funds. The main occupation of the adult females in the workhouse was the production of oakum. This arduous work involved picking old ropes to pieces to produce a loose fibre material which was then mainly used for the caulking of boats.

Outdoor Relief

In March 1837 it was ordered that all able-bodied men on outdoor relief had to attend the workhouse every morning to break stones. For each mile above two that the men had to walk to the workhouse the men were allowed half a hundredweight reduction in the amount of stones they had to break. In return for the work, as long as the men were not more than thirty minutes late, they were given their dinner. Allowed to leave as soon as their allotted work was finished, the men were paid half in kind and half in cash.

The stones, which when broken were used on the roads, were delivered by canal to the Wistow Bridge wharf from whence they were carried to the workhouse either by local carrier John

Chesterfield House. Formerly called The Firs, this eighteenth century dwelling opposite the Green was the home of the Union Medical Officer, Dr John Fewkes.

Glover, or in wheel barrows by the inmates. As the workhouse was not meant to be an easy option, in December 1840, the supplier, John Martin, was 'invited' to supply harder and larger stones! The following March Martin delivered fifty-one tons of stone valued at £15 6s.

Great Glen Parish was one of the customers for the broken stone and in December 1841 George Cooper, one of the poor law guardians, was asked to use his influence to obtain payment for a load of broken stone which had been delivered but not, as yet, paid for.

In July 1840 William Holyoak, from the parish of Keyham, refused to break his allotted portion of stones. The punishment metered out by the board was that he was put on a bread and water diet and reported to the magistrates. Holyoak, however, got one over on the board by taking out a summons against the workhouse master for depriving him of food. Benjamin Dean it seems had misunderstood the board's orders and had refused Holyoak even bread and water. The magistrate found in Holyoak's favour and Dean was cautioned.

Workhouse Administration

In September 1836 Mr Aldridge, civil registrar and relieving officer for the Tilton area, was granted a week's leave of absence while he was on service with the Leicestershire Yeomanry Cavalry. Although this leave was granted, in the margin of the minute book Assistant Poor Law Commissioner Richard Hall wrote that it should never be allowed again. The matter was resurrected the following June when Mr F. Lewis, Poor Law Commissioner, wrote to Colonel Keck telling him that although Aldridge could continue in the Yeomanry he had to put his duties as Relieving Officer first.

In November 1836 Catherine Denshaw, an inmate of the workhouse, was reported to be 'at times visited with an aberration of interlect'. A transfer to the County Lunatic Asylum was discussed, but in the event she stayed and a 'shell waistcoat' was provided for when she was violent. On the night of Monday 27 November some of Denshaw's friends battered in the workhouse door and forced Dean to release Denshaw from the solitary confinement in which she had been put.

A reward of twenty guineas was offered and advertisements, for information leading to the arrest of the people involved, placed in the local press. Two men from Newton Harcourt, Charles King and George Wheat were arrested on suspicion of the deed but had to be released due to lack of satisfactory evidence. Poor Catherine was removed to the asylum on 10 December. In January 1841 Catherine's husband, William, one of the many framework knitters whose pay was so low that their income was 'inequal to their wants', caused a minor riot in the house. Taken before the magistrates he was ordered to pay for the six shillings worth of damage which he had done.

Examples of the Poor Law in action

One of the main planks in the Poor Law Act was the idea that people should be responsible for their own families and not depend on the parish for support. An idea of the provisions of the Act can be seen from the following potted case histories in which we see it was not just children who had to be looked after but also parents.

In 1836 the payment of one shilling a week to Mary Denshire for the maintenance of her illegitimate child was discontinued as she refused to hand the child over to the father who was prepared to look after it. In February 1837 James Norfolk, shoemaker, was ordered to be responsible for the support of his father. In July 1837 John Coley ran away from the workhouse, deserting his wife and five children. The Union instituted proceedings against him and a warrant was issued for his arrest. On 28 February 1840 Sarah Holyoak, a single girl who was pregnant, applied for relief. The guardians having 'enquired diligently as to the father' found that he was Thomas Lambert, a tailor. Taken before the magistrates he was ordered to reimburse the Union for the maintainance of his child.

In January 1837 Mr Aldridge was ordered to go to Shepshed to see Sarah Mound (alias Haddon) to recover the amount of relief paid by the parish of Newton Harcourt for the support of her husband. In November of the same year Sarah Gamble was refused relief as she was living with her son who could provide for her.

In November 1840 a warrant was taken out for the arrest of forty-two year old Edward Muggleton on account of his deserting his child leaving it chargable to the parish. Not only that but when the relieving officer called on Muggleton he had been met with physically violence, an action for which Muggleton receive 21 days imprisonment with hard labour. It was, however, agreed that the case stand for one week while arrangements were made for the relief of his two children at the workhouse. He was taken to the house on the Saturday but escaped over the wall the following Monday. Muggleton was a regular in the workhouse being re-admitted in February 1843.

In May 1837 an order was made for eighty-four year old Elizabeth Fox of Illston to enter the house. The poor lady had no friends and no person would consent to look after her 'at any price'. In September 1842 Sarah Ann Holyoak was deemed too ill to remain in the house and was sent home.

The Last Days of the Great Glen Workhouse

In November 1839 Robert Haymes agreed with the parish officers of Glen to purchase the parish cottages for £490. A year later, in November 1840, the deal still had not been finalised with Haymes refusing to complete the purchase unless certain unnamed tasks were performed. In 1846 the workhouse was sold and the inmates transferred to the new Billesdon Union workhouse which had cost £3300 to build. At a vestry meeting on 27 August 1846 the former Glen workhouse was sold and the mortgagees - Henry Frederick Coleman, Robert Haymes, executors of the late John Ragg and John Grain were repaid.

Cricks Retreat

In the 1860s, Thomas Crick, born in 1803 in Leicester's Peacock Lane, moved to Rupert's Rest, Main Street. A boot and shoe manufacturer, Crick is remembered for inventing the method of riveting soles to the boot from the inside.

In 1871, in memory of his wife Elizabeth, he erected a row of ten cottages, just off London Road, which were named Crick's Retreat. Built to provide a free residence for his relatives and other poor persons 'of good character and advanced age whose income was so small that payment of rent would place it out of their power to have proper comforts and necessities in their declining years', the inhabitants were also expected to have led 'honest, sober and industrious lives and not to have been reduced to poverty though any fault of their own'.

Men had to be over 60 and women over 55 with an income not exceeding £20. They were not allowed to marry without the consent of the governing body, nor could they entertain lodgers without permission.

The residents were each paid 2s 6d a week and issued with fifty-two hundredweight of coal and fourteen pounds of candles a year. They were not to absent themselves for more than three nights in any month without permission, nor were they allowed to carry out any trade or business from the Retreat. They had to keep their houses clean, not annoy or inconvenience their fellow inmates, nor keep any animals. The porter's wife had to look after the gardens and paths as well as nursing any inmate who became sick.

In 1957 the houses were let by the Market Harborough Council for small rents before being restored in 1994 and sold as private dwellings.

In 1874 Crick had the east window in the south aisle of St Wilfrids, Kibworth, depicting the four evangelists, erected in memory of his wife and son. Thomas Crick himself died in 1879 and a plaque was erected to his memory in St Martins, Leicester. It reads: *In memory / Thomas Crick / A resident for many years in / St Martins Parish and a / Benefactor of St Martins Church. / Born November 3 1803 / Died March 6 1879.*

The carving on the gable of Crick's Retreat showing a cobbler, Thomas Crick's trade, working at his last.

Chapter 6

Communications

Pre-Turnpike Roads

The original liability for the maintenance of the highways, as laid down by the 1285 Statute of Winchester, was upon the holders of the land over which the roads passed. In 1555 this responsibility was transferred to the parish with the liability of every parishioner to provide four days labour and, those who had them, horses and carts for the same number of days. This statute labour system was satisfactory while the traffic in the parish was mostly local, for obviously the parishioners did not mind repairing the roads which were useful to themselves. Until the late seventeenth century travel was either on foot or by horseback with heavy goods transported by wheeled carts. Public transport in any quantity did not begin until the mid-eighteenth century.

The Turnpike Road

With the increase in the use of coaches and carriages, the upkeep of the roads became more important. To provide for the ever-increasing expense of this, the first turnpike trusts came into being in the late seventeenth century. It was, however, not until 1726 that the fifteen miles of road from Market

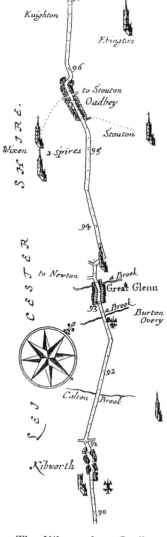

The Kibworth to Oadby road, the present A6, as it was in 1675 as shown in Ogilby's Britannia.

Harborough to Leicester were turnpiked - the first turnpike road in Leicestershire.

Roads at this time were nothing more than undefined dirt tracks, inclined towards the middle. In June 1801, George Linthwait and Thomas Roe were reimbursed for 'rampering' Burton Lane, an area of twenty-four acres. Bordered with ditches - hedges and fences are mainly of post-enclosure origin - the onus was on the occupiers of the land bordering the road to keep the ditches clear so as to allow free drainage. Nevertheless, heavy rain caused havoc. In December 1801, for instance, the flooding was so bad that it took nine days to drain the road.

The concept behind the turnpikes was that the upkeep of the road would be paid for by the users, who had to pay a toll every time they travelled. However, as most of the income went on administration the privatisation of the roads was a financial failure. By 1836, the expenditure on the Harborough to Leicester section of the road, £7,044, was far in excess of the income of £3,862. In an effort to balance the books a levy was raised on the richer inhabitants of the parish. Although very few records of these levies survive those that do give us an idea as to the wealth of the families in the village at this time. One levy which does survive is that for 1779 in which Sir George Robinson, lord of the manor, is recorded as paying seven shillings. The man given the highest assessment was Edward Linthwait who was taxed at eleven shillings and sixpence.

Glen's first collector of tolls was John Coulson who worked from the toll gate on the Oadby side of the junction of London Road and Gorse Lane. Coulson's successor, local man William Palmer, was held in high respect and on his death, in December 1768, the curate referred to him as 'the honest keeper of the Oadby turnpike". The next toll collector was Edward Mortimore who resigned, due to ill health and old age, in 1783. He was followed in the post by Daniel Clarke.

An enigmatic entry in the trustees' accounts for May 1796 concerns the then keeper, Thomas Elliot, who was given fifty shillings as compensation for having to keep 'moving backward and forwards'. In March 1802 he was paid an extra guinea a year in lieu of the previous custom of the Glen tollgate keeper taking the summer crop from a piece of Sir George Robinson's land which had usually been let to the gatekeeper.

Inns

The introduction of regular stage coach services in 1760 and the advent of the mail coach in 1785 greatly increased the business of Glen's two inns - the Greyhound and the Crown. It is possible that the Greyhound may incorporate a sixteenth century building, the oak timbers of which are still visible inside the walls carrying the beams and floors. The inn got its name from the Neale family, lords of the manor in the late sixteenth and early seventeenth centuries, whose arms were three greyhounds. In Ogilby's *Britannia* of 1675, the inn is referred to as the Halfway House - due to it being $91\frac{1}{2}$ miles equidistant from London and Manchester.

Although the present Crown was built in the late eighteenth century, a deed of 1675 mentions the Crown messuage as being held by George Woodcock as part of Sir Richard Halford's property in Great Glen. Twenty years later, in 1695, it was being run by Valentine Howes of Newton Harcourt. Halford was an ardent royalist and it is of no surprise that he named his inn in recognition of the Restoration.

That the publicans did not get it all their way is clear for, in 1789, the two local innkeepers complained to the trustees of the turnpike that, because of the system whereby toll tickets were

The Greyhound Inn.

54

The Crown Inn.

only valid on the day of issue, the inns' overnight guests had to pay two lots of tolls. Although the trustees sympathized they were not prepared to change the rules.

Repair of the Turnpike

The people responsible for the upkeep of the of parish roads were the waywardens or over-seers of the highway. The holders of the office were required to be either the owners of an estate with a value of at least ten pounds within the parish or occupiers of property with a yearly value of at least thirty pounds.

In 1731 part of the road between Glen and Oadby was repaired at the cost of one shilling and sixpence a yard. For this work labourers from the parish were assigned 'duty work' and paid six shillings a week. In order to ensure that the men fulfilled their duties they were only paid five shillings at the end of each week and, as long as they had not missed more than one day's

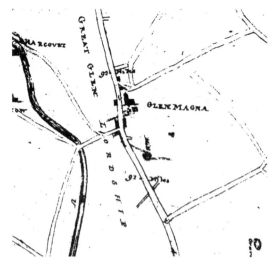

The Great Glen section of the 1813 map of the Harborough to Leicester turnpike road. (By permission of the Leicestershire Record Office)

work in five, they were paid the surplus at the end of September. They were, however, allowed an extra three days off, if needed, to get in their own harvest.

That not everybody partook willingly of the duty work can be seen from the fact that in 1735 William Cooke was asked to make monthly lists of teams which had been 'difficult or negligent' of fulfilling their legal requirement. By June 1736 it was reported that the Glen work had been completed having used 5,427 loads of gravel. Two years later William Cooper was given a thirty pound gratuity as thanks for the time and effort which he had put into the work on the road.

In 1734, 3,000 loads of gravel, at $2^1/2d$ a load, were extracted from pits in Burton Overy. The following year, under the supervision of William Cooper, John Day and James Chapman, two hundred yards of the road from the Burton boundary were layered by gravel from this pit. As can be imagined, this constant traffic going over the parish fields caused no little resentment and in 1735 three Burton landholders, John Voss, John Welby and John Newton, were prosecuted for obstructing the carts carrying the gravel for the road.

The same year, the trustees of the turnpike ordered that a search should be made for a source of gravel in Glen. One site was found on Long Close, land belonging to William Cooper, who, in 1743, received six guineas as compensation for damage done to his land caused by the extraction of the gravel. A smaller pit was dug on land occupied by Elizabeth Bell, who, in

November 1746, was paid ten shillings for supplying materials for the road.

In February 1754 a new layer of Burton gravel was laid from Windmill Lane End (the present Orchard Lane) to the border with Burton Overy, and from the church to the top of the next hill leading towards Oadby. From thereon to the Oadby border gravel from Oadby was used.

An insight as to how the roads in the eighteenth century were repaired can be seen from the turnpike account books. In 1783 Thomas Cooper was paid 10s 6d for thorns which were used to pack the ruts. In 1801 forty loads of 'riddlings' were used for paving the streets and the workhouse yard. *Riddlings* is local dialect and refers to the small stones which fell through the grid in the riddle or coarse sieve.

The men on duty work were well looked after with 'duty ale' supplied by the local inns. In 1780, for instance, Mrs Gilbert supplied ale to the value of eight shillings and sixpence, while Mrs Chapman supplied over three times as much, her account being one pound five shillings and eightpence. These entries in the accounts suggest that each innkeeper in turn was given his or her share of the parochial custom.

The turnpike trust records give an insight into the social and economic conditions of the day. An example is the entry for January 1801, when, due to the ever-rising cost of living caused by the French wars, the labourers who had been in post for at least twelve months were given a twenty-five shilling bonus. This gratuity was repeated in November 1802.

Accidents and Crime

In an attempt to cut the number of accidents caused by overloading, in 1781 the magistrates made it mandatory for lines to be painted on the carts which carried the gravel. Somewhat similar to the plimsoll line which is painted on cargo ships, the carts were not to be filled above the line.

Accidents were not confined to the carts. The many accidents involving the overturning of stagecoaches and other carriages because of overloading led, in September 1813, to the rules concerning the number of passengers and amount of luggage

This eighteenth century parish boundary stone used to stand by the side of the A6, almost opposite the entrance to the school.

carried on the sides and roofs of coaches to be strictly enforced. At the same time coach drivers were reminded that they had to keep to the left!

In June 1754 one of the village boys made a grisly discovery. While looking for bird nests, he found, in a ditch, covered with boughs, the body of a Nottingham woman named Mary Street. As well as having had her throat cut, poor Mary had been stabbed several times in the breast and face. Despite diligent investigations, the murderer was never caught.

Milestones

Although they did not become mandatory until 1773, there were milestones along the Leicester-Market Harborough road at least as early as 1747 when it was reported that they were being defaced by people who, for reasons best known to themselves, were throwing stones at them. In 1770 the milestones were checked to ensure they showed the correct distances. Although there are no surviving milestones along the Great Glen stretch of the road there is, on the east side of the road leading to Kibworth, an eighteenth century boundary stone which marks the border between Great Glen and Burton Overy. There was a signpost in place by 1803 for in October of that year Mr Harrison was paid £1 8s for painting, "writing on and setting down an oak guide-post". This may have been on the junction of the present Station Lane and the road leading to Newton Harcourt for an early nineteenth century deed records, on this site, a Guide Post Close. The following October John Cooper was paid seven shillings for repairing the sign.

The Bridge

In 1751 the bridge over the Sence, with its five small brick arches, was built to replace an older structure, for which, in 1521, Robert Green had left money for its repair. On the south side is a stone plaque which reminds the reader that 'This Bridge was built by the Trustees of the Turnpike Road in 1751'. At the same time the road over the bridge was widened by taking in 'as much of Mr Cooper's ground as he can spare'. The parapet walls were erected four feet six inches high and the mud walls belonging to George Cooper, who lived on the site of The Yews, were made good. In the Spring of 1752 a second new bridge, of two arches, was made over Burton Brook near the mill.

In 1790, as a result of the ever-increasing amount of traffic on the road, thirteen pounds was spent on widening the bridge. This work included buying sixty-five square yards of William Cooper's land, which adjoined the bridge, for £8 5s. The condition of sale being that the turnpike trustees would fence his garden with 'handsome oak posts'. At the same time the road near the Greyhound was widened by taking in land near George Robinson's house, which he gave free of charge.

In June 1818 the trustees applied to the Bishop of Lincoln for permission to widen the road by using a small piece of land belonging to and adjoining the churchyard. The intention was to avoid the two sharp turns by the church. However, as we all know, the road still takes the sharp bend. Two years later £1500 was spent on cutting the road through about one hundred yards of the crown of Glen Hill. In 1868 a further £400 was spent on widening and diverting the road twenty feet to the right.

The Canal

The sixty years between 1760 and 1820 were the era of the canals, a total of 3,000 miles being built in that time. Although plans for the Grand Junction Canal were first mooted in 1793, because of the uncertainties and inflation caused by the wars with France, it was not opened until 1805. Like the railways which were to come, canals were primarily built to carry heavy goods, such as coal, from one point in the kingdom to another. Life in Glen was hardly affected by the waterway, the numerous navvies who worked on the navigation soon passed on leaving little cultural impression on village life. The main feature of the canal as it passes through Great Glen is the aquaduct which carried the canal over a pronounced dip in the land near what has been named Aquaduct Spinney.

The Railway

The Midland Railway was extended from Leicester to Hitchin in 1854. Three years later the line was connected with London. Although only about twenty or so people living in Glen worked on the railway, one can imagine the excitement caused in the village by these giants of steam as they thundered by. The station, which opened in May 1857, closed for passenger traffic in June 1951, and is now used by a timber fencing company.

This pre-war scene shows a down train coming into Great Glen Railway Station. (Collection of Stan Allen.)

Chapter 7

Schools in Great Glen

Seventeenth Century Education

The early seventeenth century was a time of exceptional educational activity. Teaching was becoming a profession in its own right and many young men, who had been educated in local schools and had gone on to Oxford or Cambridge, returned to their home districts to teach. Great Glen had a school as early as the 1620s, for, on 15 May 1634, seventeen year old John Bale, son of Sir John Bale of Carlton Curlieu, after attending school at Glen and Stamford, went up to Sussex College, Cambridge. Two years later, on 18 January 1635–36, Edward Stapleford, who had been born in Seagrave and studied at Trinity College, Oxford, was in post as village schoolmaster after subscribing to the Three Articles, which gave evidence of his religious orthodoxy and acceptance of the royal supremacy. On 24 November 1637, Stapleford was ordained deacon, his place in the school being taken over by Thomas Oswin who subscribed on 12 April 1638.

Although there is no documentary evidence, it is quite likely that this early school, supported by the Town Land Charity, would have been held in the church north aisle. That the offices of schoolmaster and curate were often combined can be seen by the canons of 1604, which laid down that in every parish without a school the curate, if able and willing to teach, should be granted a licence before any other person.

The Early Nineteenth Century

The next reference to schools in Great Glen is found in 1818 when the Select Committee on the Education of the Poor reported that the parish had two schools - one supported by the Church of England and the other by the Methodists.

The church school dated from about 1812 when, partly from a fear of the ever-increasing numbers of dissenters, of which Great Glen contained more than a few, the National School

Society was founded with the aim of having a Church of England school in every parish. Teaching in these early schools was based on the Madras or monitorial system, whereby the older boys taught the younger ones by rote. The advantage of this, in an age when there was no state support for schools, was that the paid teaching staff could be kept to a minimum. Although there is no other reference to the Wesleyan day school, we do know that the Great Glen congregation held a Sunday School anniversary as early as 1812.

The 1833 Abstraction of Education Returns reported that there were three schools in Great Glen, mainly paid for by the parents with a small statutory government grant. There was an infant school, catering for twenty-one children; a day school for 30 boys and 10 girls: and a boarding school which catered for up to twenty children. This last school, believed to have been in what is now the Royal Oak, High Street, was run by William Edgley,

The Royal Oak, High Street. It was here that William Edgley held his school.

who had been born in the village in 1807. Edgley, who also ran a grocery business, utilised a novel method of punishment whereby the offender was made to stand on one leg on a form while holding up a Bible in one hand.

The 1841 census lists Elizabeth Brake, a 37 year old schoolmistress from Dorset. Ten years later Brake's establishment was recorded as having 6 boarders: Mary Dickins, age 12, from London; Richard Taylor, age 9 from Leicester; William and Henry Hobson, age 8 and 7, from Great Stretton; John A. Smith, age 7, from Kibworth; Edward Gill, age 8 from Leicester and Palmer Bailey, age 7, also from Leicester.

Two Sunday Schools were also reported in 1833, both supported by public collections. St Cuthbert's had 32 boys and 28 girls while the Methodists attracted 37 boys and 33 girls. These numbers show how the village was split almost in two by the schism between the established church and dissenters, a topic which is discussed in greater detail elsewhere.

The Packe School

The year 1846 was a milestone in the history of education in the village, for it was in that year that that Charles William Packe, who had become lord of the manor in 1838, built a school (the germ of the present St Cuthbert's Primary School) and schoolmaster's house in Main Street. The master's house is still standing, with the date of erection and the initials CWP. inscribed above the door.

Built to cater for 160 pupils the school displayed the Packe crests, which are now built into the wall to the left of the main entrance of the new primary school in The Chase. The crests

The former schoolmaster's house in Main Street. Built in 1846 with the initials CWP - Charles William Packe - on the gable.

Top: *Packe's school in Main Street. Built on the site of the present Fairfax Court in 1846, it was demolished in 1967. Note the crest on the gable.*
© *Glen Sense.*
Bottom: *The Packe crests once on the Main Street school and now on the primary school in the Chase.*

are(i) a lion's head erased Or collared Sable charged with three cinquefoils Ermine; (ii) on a mount Vert, a hind lodged regardant proper gorged with a ducal coronet, therefrom a line reflexed over the back Or, in front of a hawthorn tree Proper. The lion's head crest with the motto *Libertas Sub Rege Pio* (liberty under a pious king) is still used as the school motto.

Packe's school was maintained through annual subscriptions, government grants and, to a lesser extent, by the sale of the children's work. The grants, which depended on the number of children being taught, varied from £12 10s in 1861 to £81 12s in 1881. The sale of work, which consisted of needlework made by the girls, raised sums from 5s 4d in 1873 to 17s 7d in 1877. In 1903 the produce of the three weekly one and half-hour sessions of sewing brought in £1 9s 7d.

The first teachers appointed by Packe were Thomas Tailington, a thirty-year old teacher from Tutbury, Staffordshire, and Martha Newton, who had been running the previous church school. Tailington, who died in January 1868, was succeeded by James Mumford, a man of no mean musical ability, who died the following November.

In the Spring of 1868 the Reverend Dodds asked Mrs Packe if Mumford could give the children singing lessons. Mrs Packe turned down the request, saying that she disapproved of combining instruction in music with the work of the school, the belief being that schools were only there to teach reading, writing, arithmetic and the Bible. She told Dodds that as long as Mumford did what he had been employed for, she had not the slightest interest in his musical ability and that if Dodds wanted a church choir he should make arrangements for it to be taught outside school hours.[1]

One of Dodds's responsibilities was to attend the school at nine every morning in order to lead morning prayers. However, such was his lack of punctuality that his irregularity interfered with the school work, for no matter what time he turned up he expected everything to stop for prayers. By June 1868 Mumford's wife, who was employed as schoolmistress, had had

---

1. *Much of this chapter is taken from the correspondence between Dodds and Packe which is held in the Leicestershire Record Office (DE849)*

enough and complained to Packe that Dodds's behaviour was causing havoc at the school. Some days, so Mrs Mumford reported, he did not even bother to come at all, thereby putting the school to great inconvenience. Packe told the teachers that if Dodds was not there by nine they were to assume he was not coming and carry on with their classes.

In early August Dodds tried to make up the quarrel with the schoolmistress, who he said 'should be less touchy', and suggested to Mrs Packe that the time of prayers at the school should be changed to ten o'clock. This was the last straw for Mrs Packe who told Dodds in no uncertain terms that his persistent changing the times of his visits was detrimental to the running of the school. Her note to Dodds ended in a tone of exasperation - 'excuss bluntness but I have better things to do!'

The following October Dodds asked Mrs Packe if he could use the schoolroom for the annual November Feast 'as heretofore'. Although the request was initially granted, in early November, Mumford fell ill and Mrs Packe thought it best that the gay and noisy festivities of feast week should be cancelled and the school closed to visitors. In the event Mumford died and was buried on 25 November.

Held on the Monday the children's party was the first event of Glen's annual Feast Week which included a men's supper on the Tuesday, a women's tea on the Wednesday and climaxed on the Friday evening with a grand ball held in a marquee erected in front of the vicarage.

As the feast had been organised before Mumford's illness, rather than cancel the event Dodds moved the venue of the festivities from the schoolrooms so that the children, who had been looking forward to the annual party, would not be disappointed. In spite of Mrs Packe's objections Dodds felt that he was in no way being disrespectful to Mumford, for "had he not made regular visits to the dying man and lodged his daughters at the vicarage when they had come to visit their sick father?"

As Mumford had been in the village only a few months, Dodds considered that a long period of mourning would not be natural and that cancelling the feast would not endear Mumford's memory to the children, quite possibly the reverse. In spite of the funeral being over and all the family out of the parish at the time of the party, Mrs Packe still expressed amazement that Dodds, instead of cancelling the party, had actually promoted the gaeity of the children. Her view was that the children had just lost one of 'their best and kindest friends' and felt that it was right, as a mark of respect to Mrs Mumford, to prohibit the use of the school room for the festivities.

The relationship between Dodds and the school went from bad to worse and in February 1869 his behaviour became almost too much for the teachers to bear. One Sunday Dodds refused to go to the schoolroom to lead the prayers at the Sunday school, sending the teachers a message to the effect that as he had not received permission to enter the school the assembled children would have to come to the church. In spite of Matthew Pywell, the Sunday school teacher, going to Dodds with the message that they were ready for prayers and were waiting at the school, Dodds still did not go and Pywell, a shoe-maker by trade who was paid two shillings a week to teach the Sunday school, had to lead the prayers himself. Understandably the teachers found it strange that Dodds insisted in visiting the school daily but refused to come on Sunday! Mrs Mumford, who after the death of her husband carried on as headmistress, wrote to Mrs Packe suggesting that as Dodds wanted the Sunday school to be his then the teachers should have the day school with Dodds's services dispensed with altogether.

Mrs Packe again wrote to Dodds requesting him to discontinue his visits to her school, telling him at the same time that she was writing to the school informing them of her decision. She ended her letter with the hope that Dodds would not continue on a course of conduct which she found 'highly objectionable in every point of view, particularly as it was vexatious and annoying to the teachers and children'.

Dodds countered by reminding Mrs Packe of her note of the previous November, in which she had stated that 'no school or any other meeting will be held in the schoolrooms until further notice'. This prohibition, so Dodds contended, had never been withdrawn so he was under the impression that he was not even to hold Sunday school in the schoolroom again. He went on to ask Mrs Packe if she really thought that his presence in the school was, as she had told him, 'extremely injurious' to the children especially as he had never had any complaints from the parents. Dodds ended his note by saying that he thought that Mrs Mumford was glad of his support and that he expected to get on well with Edward Paulson, the new headmaster.

Relations did not improve and in March Mrs Packe told Dodds that any more visits to the school would be considered a trespass on her property. The same day she advised Mrs Mumford, who had been saying that she feared Dodds was 'not quite right at times', to be very careful in what she said to or about him to anyone and not to write anything to him or of him to anyone but herself. Mrs Packe also advised Mrs Mumford to keep the front doors locked and that if Dodds called at the school she was to go out the back door and meet him in the front porch. There she was to tell him that she dare not admit him on pain of Mrs Packe's displeasure.

In time the misunderstandings between incumbent and school were ironed out and Dodds was again admitted to the school.

Ten years later, in January 1878, Dodds again withdrew his support of the school, complaining that he was being 'gagged'. For Charles Packe this was the last straw and in a tone of exasperation he wrote to Dodds reminding him that this was not the first time that he had renounced teaching in the school. He went on to say that even if Dodds did feel aggrieved personally it did not seem either Christian or logical to make the innocent children suffer for it. Packe ironically ended his letter with the comment that he supposed that Dodds considered that his instruction in the school did some good and that no doubt he (Dodds) knew best how his conscience excused him from shirking his duty.

In April 1871, William Henry Fancourt, was appointed headmaster. A Londoner, born in April 1847, on Easter Day 1883 he married local girl Mary Morris Thompson. Fancourt's salary at the time was £75 a year, while the schoolmistress, Sally Ann Hall, was receiving £25 annually. By 1903 Fancourt's salary had risen to £125.

In March 1892 the managers of the school discussed the

possibility of giving the school board status but, because of its poor financial position, they decided to continue on a subscription basis. However, in 1897, under the Voluntary School Act, the school did join the Leicester Associated Board of Education, a forerunner of the Leicestershire Education Authority.

In November 1892 the relatively progressive school managers decreed that corporal punishment was to be only resorted to only as a last resort, and even then the punishment was not to be metered out straight after the offence, in front of the class, but at the close of school and away from the other pupils.

Money continued to be a problem, so much so that, in 1894, Packe, feeling that he could not continue to act as treasurer of an indebted institution, resigned. He did, however, continue supporting the school, for in October 1894 he paid for the school's six pit closets to be converted to earth closets. The toilets were arranged to be emptied weekly by local builder John Batchelor, a task for which he was paid two shillings a week. In 1900 the school inspectors reported that the classroom was too small, smokey, badly ventilated and unsuitable for use.

After World War II the Victorian building became inadequate with some of the 128 pupils having to be taught over the road in the village hall. During the 1960s, with the population of the village growing fast, from 1,400 in 1961 to 2,716 in 1971, the need for a new school became even more urgent until, in 1967, the present building was erected in The Chase.

Great Glen Hall was built by William Burton, for Sir George Robinson in the 1820s. In 1838 it was purchased by Charles Packe, MP for South Leicestershire and Great Glen's new lord of the manor. The grounds are still as they must have looked over a century ago.

The Heart of Albion Press catalogue
now includes details of no less than
forty-five other titles on Leicestershire
local history - and many further books,
booklets and electronic publications on
other subjects.

Please phone, write or e-mail for a
copy of the current catalogue - or visit
our WWW on-line catalogue.

Heart of Albion Press

2 Cross Hill Close, Wymeswold,
Loughborough, LE12 6UJ

Phone: 01509 880725

E-mail: bobtrubs@gmtnet.co.uk

On-line catalogue: http://www.gmtnet.co.uk/
indigo/albion/hoaphome.htm